A+ books

## Words I Know

# A Hat Full of Adjectives

by Bette Blaisdell

Content Consultant:
Terry Flaherty, PhD
Professor of English
Minnesota State University, Mankato

CAPSTONE PRESS
a capstone imprint

T010922

A+ Books are published by Capstone Press,
1710 Roe Crest Drive, North Mankato, Minnesota 56003
www.capstonepub.com

**Library of Congress Cataloging-in-Publication Data**
Blaisdell, Bette.
  A hat full of adjectives / by Bette Blaisdell.
     pages cm.—(A+ books. Words i know)
  Summary: "Full-color photographs and rhyming text introduce and
define a variety of adjectives"—Provided by publisher.
  ISBN 978-1-4765-3937-9 (library binding)
  ISBN 978-1-4765-5097-8 (paperback)
  ISBN 978-1-4765-5942-1 (eBook PDF)
1. English language—adjective—Juvenile literature. I. Title.
PE1241.B48 2014
425'.5—dc23                          2013035671

**Editorial Credits**
Jill Kalz, editor; Juliette Peters, designer; Svetlana Zhurkin, media researcher; Kathy McColley, production specialist

**Photo Credits**
iStockphotos: wdstock, 8; Shutterstock: 2xSamara, 10, AKaiser, 2–3, 4–5 (back), 32, Andrey Arkusha, 22 (top),
Anneka, cover, Annette Shaff, 28 (top), Bernhard Richter, 15 (bottom), bikeriderlondon, 24 (bottom), Brocreative,
4 (bottom), buruhtan, 26, Chen WS, 22 (bottom), Dan Breckwoldt, 5 (right), Danny Smythe, 27 (top right), Denis
Trofimov, 13 (top), Dusan Zidar, 24 (top), Elena Schweitzer, 18 (top), Elenamiv, 21 (bottom), Florin Stana, 25 (top),
Givaga, 19 (middle), GVictoria, 5 (left), Igor Terekhov, 14 (bottom left), Ivonne Wierink, 6–7, Jan S., 12–13 (back),
Jean-Edouard Rozey, 18 (bottom), Jerry Horbert, 28 (bottom), JonMilnes, 25 (bottom), Joy Fera, 16 (bottom),
Kenishirotie, 27 (bottom), Kokhanchikov, 29, kostrez, 9 (bottom), Leena Robinson, 4 (top), M. Unal Ozmen, 1,
Madlen, 27 (top left), mexrix, 14 (bottom right), mycola, 20 (bottom), Nailia Schwarz, 9 (top), naluwan, 11 (top),
Norman Chan, 12 (right), OLJ Studio, 12 (left), Paulo M. F. Pires, 16 (top), Photo Fun, 14 (top), Rob Hainer, 23
(bottom), Rohit Seth, 21 (top), Rosli Othman, 11 (bottom), saiko3p, 19 (top), Sanjay Deva, 23 (top), Sergey Novikov,
20 (top), Steven Russell Smith Photos, 19 (bottom), Svetlana Valoueva, 13 (bottom), Varina and Jay Patel, 15 (top),
Vilainecrevette, 17, Zurijeta, 30–31

**Note to Parents, Teachers, and Librarians**
This Words I Know book uses full-color photographs and a nonfiction format to introduce the concept of language
and parts of speech. *A Hat Full of Adjectives* is designed to be read aloud to a pre-reader or to be read independently
by an early reader. Photographs help listeners and early readers understand the text and concepts discussed. The book
encourages further learning by including the following sections: Table of Contents, Read More, and Internet Sites.
Early readers may need assistance using these features.

# Table of Contents

# What's an Adjective?

How many kids are on the swing? *Three*! What kind of ice cream does Maya like? *Peppermint*! Which dog is Luke's? The *spotted* dog!

You've just met some adjectives.

An **adjective** is a part of speech that describes a person, place, or thing. It adds detail.

Adjectives may tell how something looks, smells, tastes, feels, or sounds. They may answer these questions: How many? How big? What kind? Which? Adjectives usually come before the objects they describe in a sentence.

**What silly, fluffy adjectives will you pull out of _your_ hat?**

# Beyond the Rainbow

You've seen red, blue, yellow, and green.
How many other colors have you seen?

mustard
coral
emerald
cocoa

violet
lavender
jade
tomato

aqua
lime
cobalt
crimson

magenta
copper
turquoise
lemon

# Size It Up

Super big or super small,
these fun size words will cover it all.

mammoth
colossal
jumbo
gigantic

enormous
gargantuan
massive
titanic

mini
**tiny**
itty-bitty
**teeny**

wee
petite
**pint-size**

**teensy**

# How Do You Feel?

How do you feel about summer or school?
Or ice cream? Snakes? A day at the pool?

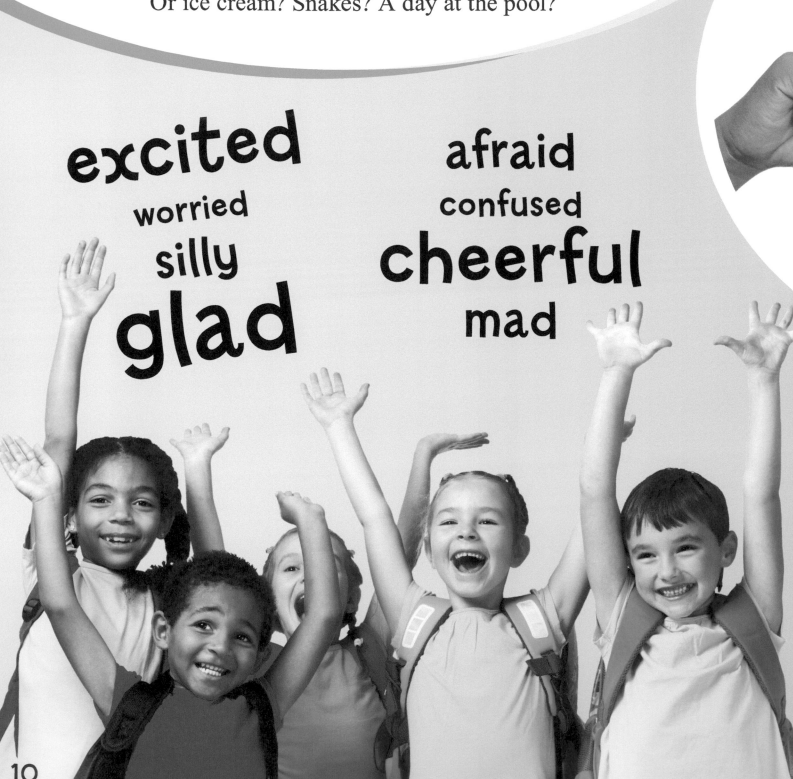

excited
worried
silly
glad

afraid
confused
cheerful
mad

grumpy
scared
**goofy**
sleepy

**bored**
gloomy
**puzzled**
weepy

# Your Listening Ears

Think of all the sounds you hear,
the sounds that tickle your ticklish ear.

bubbling

# gurgling

purring

cooing

blaring

thundering

# hissing

booing

screeching
**buzzing**
snapping
**stuttering**

humming
crying
**barking**
muttering

# Not the Same

Opposites are different as can be.
If one bird is caged, the other is free!

boiling/freezing

black/white

sweet/sour

heavy/light

wild/tame

dirty/clean

swift/slow
friendly/mean

# What's Your Speed?

When you move, when you go,
are you fast, or are you slow?

speedy
rapid
supersonic
quick

hasty
zippy
snappy
brisk

poky plodding

sluggish crawling

lazy

tardy shuffling dawdling

# By the Numbers

"How many?" is a question we often ask,
and these adjectives are up to the task.

twelve
**eighteen**
every
**seven**

**many**
one hundred
less
**eleven**

most

each

# forty

more

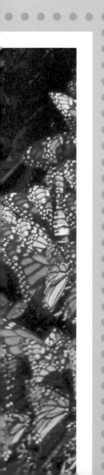

# few five

some

# sixty-four

# Weather Report

What will the weather bring today?
Will you need boots and mittens to play?

frosty
blazing
humid
**wintry**

frigid
icy
**sizzling**

**fiery**

nippy
**chilly**
sweltering
**muggy**

blistering

steaming

frozen

**sunny**

# Who Are You?

What kind of kid are you?
Helpful? Kind? Honest and true?

brave

bubbly

wise

dramatic

generous

smart

healthy

athletic

stubborn
funny
thoughtful
**brainy**

bold
**fearless**
timid
**zany**

23

# The Shape of Things

These words describe how objects look.
Which word best describes this book?

round

square

pointed

hollow

crooked   flat   wide

shallow

narrow
curved
straight

steep

skinny
rippled
thick

deep

# Taste Test

Grab your fork, and dig right in.
So many foods, where do you begin?

spicy
juicy
stringy
delicious

salty greasy tart
nutritious

mushy
chewy
bitter
**pasty**

**sticky**
rotten
**crunchy**
**tasty**

# Keep in Touch

Your sense of touch helps you know
if something's hot or cold as snow.

slippery
**fuzzy**
slick
**bumpy**

cuddly
smooth
**prickly**
lumpy

sharp   shaggy   itchy

grimy

grubby

damp

rough

slimy

# What a Day!

Was your day better than just OK?
Then try these words. They're fun to say!

excellent
wonderful
spectacular
great

fantastic
terrific
superb
first-rate

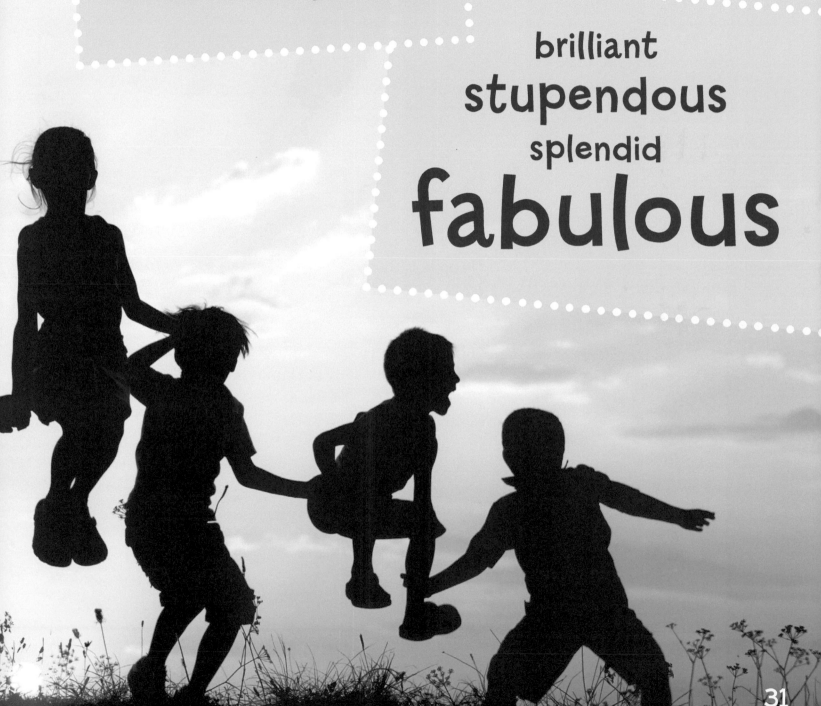

awesome
amazing
remarkable
marvelous

brilliant
stupendous
splendid
fabulous

# Read More

**Carter, Andrew.** *Adjectives.* Grammar Ray: A Graphic Guide to Grammar. New York: Alphabet Soup, 2010.

**Cleary, Brian. P.** *Quirky, Jerky, Extra-Perky: More about Adjectives.* Words Are Categorical. Minneapolis: Millbrook Press, 2007.

**Fandel, Jennifer.** *What Is an Adjective?* Parts of Speech. North Mankato, Minn.: Capstone Press, 2013.

**Riggs, Kate.** *Adjectives.* Grammar Basics. Mankato, Minn.: Creative Education, 2013.

# Internet Sites

FactHound offers a safe, fun way to find Internet sites related to this book. All of the sites on FactHound have been researched by our staff.

Here's all you do:

Visit *www.facthound.com*

Type in this code: 9781476539379

Super-cool stuff! Check out projects, games and lots more at **www.capstonekids.com**